From the Farm to the Table
Bees

by

Kathy Coatney

CONTENTS

Dedication

To Beekeeper Pat, with thanks for his time and expertise.

Acknowledgements

Many thanks to those who have assisted me with this project. Georgia Bockoven, who put the idea in my head. Patti Thurman, and Jenny Reilly, who consulted and proofread for me. To my email check-in pals, Jennifer Skullestad and Lisa Sorensen, a huge thanks. Luann Erickson, Susan Crosby, Karol Black, and Tammy Lambeth, who critiqued and supported me through the process. To the Redding Lunch Bunch, Libby, Shari, Dianna, Lisa, Terry, and Patti, you're the best. To my family, Nick, Wade and Devin, Collin and Ellis, Jake and Emily, Allie and Russell. You all have been my inspiration. Thank you. I never would have made it without you.

Note to parents and teachers: The words underlined are second-grade vocabulary words. A list of the words used can be found at the end of the book.

Also By

Thank you for reading **From the Farm to the Table Bees**, book 2 in **From the Farm to the Table series** of picture books.

I love hearing from my fans. You can contact me through my website: www.kathycoatney.com.

From the Farm to the Table

From the Farm to the Table Dairy
From the Farm to the Table Bees
From the Farm to the Table Olives
From the Farm to the Table Potatoes
From the Farm to the Table Almonds
From the Farm to the Table Beef

Stand Alone Picture Book
Dad's Girls

From the Farm to the Table Bees

Beekeeper Pat with his bee colonies

Beekeeper Pat is an insect guy. Before he became an insect guy he was a bike guy. He owned a bike shop near the ocean, where he sold and repaired bicycles.

Beekeeper Pat with his bees

One day a man offered to trade him a <u>colony</u> of bees for a bike. He agreed and took the bees home. Before he knew it, he spent more time working with the bees than the bikes.

Bees making honey in the honeycomb

Bees became Beekeeper Pat's favorite insects. He was <u>impressed</u> that they were such hard workers, and he admired the important work that they do. Bees make honey, and beeswax, and they also <u>pollinate</u>.

Prune blossoms

Pollination is when the bees transfer pollen from one plant to another plant and fertilize it. This is very important for growing a variety of crops, from almonds to zucchini squash.

Bees make honey that Beekeeper Pat loves to eat. He drizzles honey on his cereal and spoons it into his tea. He <u>especially</u> likes it spread on top of his oatmeal for breakfast.

Almond blossoms

Bees make different kinds of honey by collecting <u>nectar</u> from different types of flowers. Wildflower, sweet clover, alfalfa, orange blossom and sage honey are just a few. They also make almond honey, but it is bitter and icky to eat.

Worker bees working in the hive making honey

Beekeeper Pat also likes bees because they are very friendly, and they <u>communicate</u> with each other constantly.

Worker bees in the colony <u>communicating</u>

When the <u>worker bees</u> find pollen or nectar, they return to the colony and begin dancing around and around in circles. The dancing excites the other bees and tells them the dancing bee found food. They can also smell the pollen or nectar on the dancing bee.

Worker bee collecting nectar from a melon blossom

Beekeeper Pat knows all about bees. Bees fly long <u>distances</u>, 3–5 miles a day, in search of nectar from the flowers. Nectar is the sugary water that is a carbohydrate for the bees.

Bottles of sugar water on the colonies

Carbohydrates are a kind of food that <u>satisfies</u> the bees' need for energy, just like it does for people. People eat different carbohydrates than bees do. Foods like brown rice, whole wheat bread, and beans are good sources of carbohydrates and energy for people.

Worker bees collecting pollen from a sunflower

To pollinate, bees land on a flower. Their feet touch <u>pollen sacs</u>. Pollen sacs are on the inside of the flower. Bees have hair on their legs, and they pack the pollen onto the hair to take back to the colony. When a bee moves to the next flower, it carries the pollen with it and pollinates the next flower.

Worker bee with pollen packed on its legs

   Pollen is a protein powder made by the flowers and comes in various colors, from blues, to reds, to yellows. The <u>larvae</u> or baby bees eat lots and lots of pollen because they need protein to grow.

Worker bee covered in pollen and back legs full of pollen

Most baby bees are born in the spring when there are plenty of flowers to produce pollen to feed them.

Beekeeper Pat inspecting a colony

The bees raise their larvae and store their honey in the colonies. Beekeeper Pat <u>inspects</u> the colonies regularly to make sure they are solid and secure. A strong colony has eight to ten pounds of bees. There are about 3,500 bees in a pound, and there are about 35,000 bees in a colony.

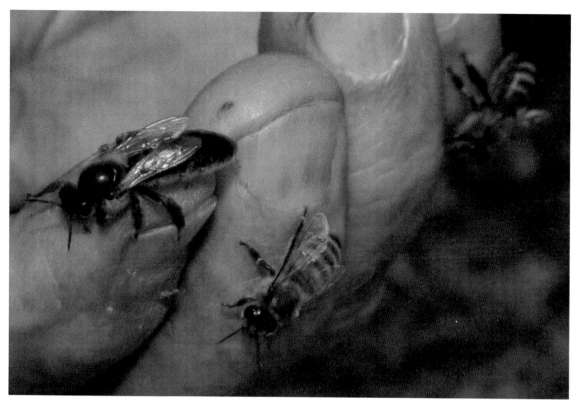

Beekeeper Pat has a queen bee on his first finger and worker bee on the others

In each colony, there are three types of bees: a <u>queen bee</u>, worker bees and <u>drone</u> <u>bees</u>. The queen bee and the worker bees are all female. The drone bees are male, and their only job is to mate with the queen.

A worker bee collecting pollen

Worker bees have many <u>chores</u>. They collect the nectar to make honey, and they produce the honeycomb. They also feed the queen bee and the larvae, guard the entrance to the hive and keep it cool by fanning their wings. Did you know a bee's wings beat 11,400 times a minute, and the beating of their wings is what makes them buzz?

19

Worker bees in the colony

Beekeeper Pat has 6,000 colonies of bees. That is 210 million bees he watches over all year long.

Bee colonies in an almond orchard in February

   Beekeeper Pat moves the colonies in his truck to places they will have food. In February, they go to almond orchards. In March, they go to prune, peach and citrus orchards. In summer, the colonies stay near alfalfa fields, and in winter, they are on <u>meadows</u> where cattle graze.

21

Worker bees in the colony making beeswax

Beekeeper Pat's colonies are rectangular boxes built of wood. Inside each colony is a group of many hexagonal cells. These cells are made from <u>beeswax</u>, and they are called a <u>honeycomb</u>.

Honeycomb from a bee colony

A honeycomb has very, very thin walls that are only 1/500 of an inch thick. That is thinner than a sheet of paper. But even being so thin, the honeycomb is <u>incredibly</u> strong. It supports 25 times the bee's own weight.

Beekeeper Pat opening a bee colony

Beekeeper Pat wears a special <u>beekeeper</u> <u>suit</u> that is snow white. The suit is white because white is difficult for the bees to see. He also wears a <u>beekeeper's veil</u> that is a white hat with mesh netting attached to it.

Beekeeper Pat uses smoke to calm the bees

The veil and suit protect Beekeeper Pat from being stung by the bees. He also uses smoke to calm the bees.

25

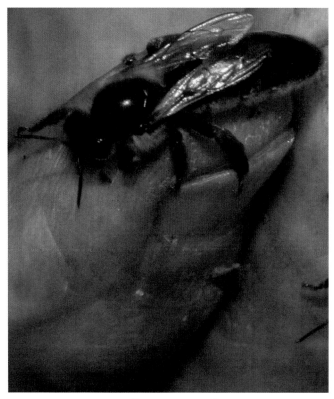
Queen Bee

Beekeeper Pat loves queen bees, and he raises them for other beekeepers. A queen bee has a very important job. She keeps the colony together. If the queen becomes less productive or dies, the whole colony will fall apart.

Colony of bees at a sunflower field

In northern California, where Beekeeper Pat lives, the weather is ideal to raise queen bees. They like the mild winters and warm days.

Sugar water Beekeeper Pat is feeding his bees

Beekeepers across the United States buy bees from northern California, but the area lacks an adequate source of nectar. This means Beekeeper Pat has to feed his bees sugar water to <u>satisfy</u> their appetites.

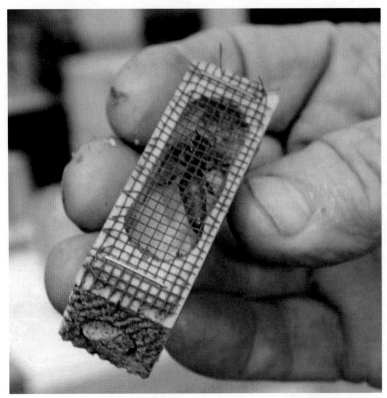
Queen bee in a box to be sold

Every March, Beekeeper Pat begins to produce queen bees. He does this by tricking the worker bees into thinking they don't have a queen so that they will make lots of <u>queen cells</u>. A cell is where the queen stays until she hatches.

Beekeeper Pat checks the colony for queen bees

The bees make thousands and thousands and thousands of these cells. The cells are put into little wooden containers that are about the size of a lunch box.

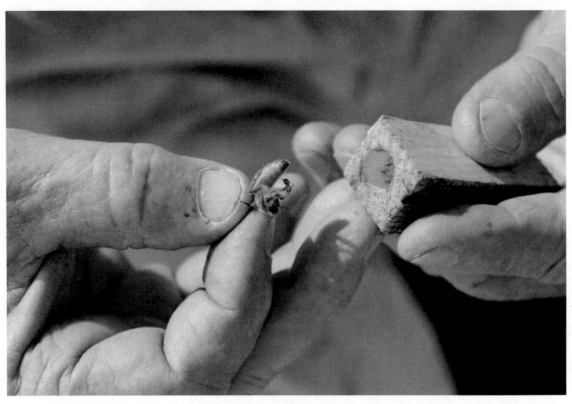
Queen Bee being put in a box to be sold

When a cell hatches, it looks like a butterfly coming out of a cocoon. In about 10 days, the queen lays eggs. Once she lays the eggs, Beekeeper Pat captures her, and then she is sold.

Melons are one of the foods bees pollinate

Bees are very important. Many of the foods we eat are dependent on bees for pollination. One third of the food we eat in the United States depends on pollination from bees.

Beekeeper Pat riding his bike

So, the next time you're out riding your bike and <u>notice</u> a bee buzzing past, Beekeeper Pat says to remember that bee is hard at work making food that you love to eat.

The End

Vocabulary List

Chores
Communicate
Distances
Especially
Impressed
Incredibly
Inspects
Meadows
Notice Satisfy

Author Biography

Kathy Coatney has worked as a freelance photojournalist for 35 years, starting in parenting magazines, then fly fishing, and finally specializing in agriculture. Her work can be seen in the California Farm Bureau magazine, *Ag Alert* and *West Coast Nut* magazine.

Visit her website at: www.KathyCoatney.com

Made in the USA
Middletown, DE
22 April 2025

74619862R00022